ECONOMIC LIBERALIZATION, INFORMALIZATION OF LABOUR AND SOCIAL PROTECTION IN INDIA

ECONOMIC LIBERALIZATION, INFORMALIZATION OF LABOUR AND SOCIAL PROTECTION IN INDIA

S. Parasuraman

AAKAR

In Association with

ŚRUTI

Society for Rural Urban & Tribal Initiative

Economic Liberalization, Informalization of Labour and Social Protection in India
S. Parasuraman

First Published 2010

ISBN 978-93-5002-103-3

Published by
AAKAR BOOKS
28 E Pocket IV, Mayur Vihar Phase I, Delhi 110 091
Phone : 011 2279 5505 Telefax : 011 2279 5641
aakarbooks@gmail.com; www.aakarbooks.com

In association with
SRUTI
Q-1, Hauz Khas Enclave, New Delhi 110 016
Web : www.sruti.org.in
E-mail : sruti@vsnl.com

Printed at
S.N. Pritners, G-28, Sector 2, Bawana, Delhi 110 039

Contents

1

Introduction

Abstract: *Regardless of economic, social and demographic contexts and national political differences, all nation-states have embraced neo-liberal policies in order to link with international trade and competitiveness in a globalizing world. The current phase of economic slump precipitated by the excesses in the financial sector has prompted countries to fix the financial sector rather than examine development paradigms. This paper examines India's performance with economic growth and its implications to people, and the nature and extent of social protection measures put in place to address the consequences.*

From a range of experiences across the world, the words 'development' and 'displacement' have now become synonymous; as if, there can be no development without displacement—of peoples, cultures, economies, and nature. In the world of the industrial civilization, things have remained thus for a long time, and in the new context it occurs in accentuated and legitimized fashion. Economically, in the era of global capital and so-called free-markets, development with its extremely visible and dominant iconography has become but an embodiment of capital, and vice versa. Dominance of the capital–development synergy in today's globalized world has an 'absolute' and uniform surface, where shopping malls, special economic zones (SEZs), and sky-hugging towers flourish, and which increasingly seem to be rejecting the subaltern 'other' that is poor, underfed, disgruntled, and displaced, and hence, not part of this 'developed' landscape. People are made to helplessly watch their homes, agricultural fields, forests, rivers, seas, and mountains taken away (*Mausam*, 2008).

The ILO Commission on Fair Globalization (ILO, 2004) concluded that "Globalization involves changes in economic structure, relative prices, and consumption possibilities and patterns, which in turn affects peoples' jobs, livelihoods and incomes". The economic benefits and social costs of globalization are not evenly distributed among social groups. Invariably some are adversely affected, while others gain from this often intense process of change.

Several sectors of the economy and social groups were seriously impacted by the economic liberalization processes. In many countries some groups of workers have been adversely affected by trade liberalization and relocation of production to lower-wage economies. While this has so far primarily affected unskilled workers, some skilled and professional workers have also been affected by developments such as the outsourcing of software development, the increasing trade in professional services, and increased immigration of skilled professionals from developing countries. Labour displacing capital investment in the manufacturing sector, outsourcing of production processes and displacement of labour from agriculture have intensified the informalization of labour.

2

Informalization of Labour

The forces of globalization have created conditions for the informalization of labour in three ways (Sanyal and Bhattacharya, 2009):

1. The dismantling of barriers to trade and capital flows has made way for the unhindered mobility of commodity and capital (both financial and real) across national boundaries. Faced with competition at the global level, firms in the formal sector of developing economies are engaged in a battle of competitive cost cutting. They are increasingly relying on outsourcing of production processes to informal units where wage costs and costs associated with complying with labour and environmental standards are considerably lower.
2. The inflow of cheaper imports has caused a contraction of import-competing industries in the formal sector, but the expansion of the export sector has failed to generate sufficient employment to compensate for the loss. Moreover, global competition has forced domestic private as well as state enterprises to raise labour productivity and adopt lean production methods involving large-scale retrenchment of workers. Further, the neo-liberal focus on fiscal discipline and inflation-targeting has

eroded the power of the state to otherwise create employment.

3. The classic paradigm of economic growth in developing countries was based on the pre-supposition that modern economy would expand by breaking up traditional (pre-capitalist) economies, transferring both economic resources and labourers from the traditional to the modern economy. Yet, the experience of economic growth in developing countries shows that while the capitalist economy did expand by breaking up traditional economies, it did so by transferring resources, not labourers. As a result, a "surplus" labour force emerged consisting of dispossessed producers whose traditional livelihoods were destroyed but who were not absorbed in the modern sector.

In an era of heightened global competition, large enterprises profit from the existence of surplus labour pools because they help minimize labour costs, are unprotected, and increase flexibility (Rudra, 2002). However, in most contexts, a significant part of this "surplus" labour force fell back on agriculture dominated by peasant production—the largest surviving traditional (pre-capitalist) economy in the world. The rest of the "surplus" labour force survived on petty non-traditional manufacturing as well as service activities, most importantly, retail. Wherever the "surplus" labour force settled, the following economic characteristics emerged—(i) the clear preponderance of self-employment largely assisted by family labour, (ii) the household as a major site of production, particularly in the case of non-agricultural activities, and (iii) community or kinship networks involving trust and reciprocity in place of impersonal relations.

In India, labour can be classified in terms of:

(a) direct wage-workers in capitalist production,
(b) labour force in informal enterprises linked to the

capitalist enterprises in the formal economy through sub-contracting and putting out, and

(c) labour force in informal enterprises outside the circuit of capital.

Wage-workers in capitalist production consist of agricultural workers on capitalist farms, public sector employees and private sector non-agricultural workers. The second tier of the labour force consists mainly of a part of rural non-farm labour and urban informal labour in non-agricultural informal enterprises linked to the capitalist economy via sub-contracting as also agricultural workforce tied to agro-business enterprises through contract-farming. The third-tier of the labour force constitutes the surplus labour force which is clearly outside of capital. It consists of the rural non-farm and urban informal labour force with no direct linkages to the formal economy (Sanyal and Bhattacharya, 2009).

Globalization has its particular impact on each of these three tiers of the labour force in the Indian context. For reasons already mentioned earlier, the forces of globalization have constrained employment growth in the first tier. Public sector employment has steadily declined over the period of 1999–2005, from 19.058 million in 1999 to 18.007 million in 2005 (*Economic Survey*, 2007–2008). Private enterprises in the formal sector have generated additional employment entirely in the category of unprotected regular, casual or contract wage-workers which constitute informal employment. The workforce in the informal sector grew from 361.7m in 1999–2000 to 422.6m in 2004–2005. The emerging evidence shows that job destruction has outpaced job creation in the formal sector, forcing those thrown out of employment to eke out a living in the informal sector.

The adversely affected include those associated with uncompetitive enterprises that have been unable to survive in the face of trade liberalization or the entry of foreign firms. These enterprises include those previously highly protected by trade barriers, subsidized State enterprises, and small-

and medium-sized enterprises that had a limited capacity to adjust to a rapid liberalization of the economy. Impoverished producers of importables, whether in the urban informal economy or in agriculture, have been particularly vulnerable to the influx of cheap imports and sharp changes in the relative prices and availability of inputs. Others, who have lost out, except in countries that have experienced rapid growth, have been the poor, the assetless, the illiterate and unskilled workers, and indigenous[1] peoples. This has occurred not only as a result of the primary economic impact of globalization, but also because of its indirect effects.

NOTES

1. A particularly vulnerable group is indigenous peoples. Where their integration into the global economy has occurred without their free and prior informed consent and without adequate protection of their rights, livelihoods, and culture, they have suffered severely. In such cases, investments in extractive industries, mega-hydroelectric dams, and plantations have led to massive dislocations, disruption of livelihoods, ecological degradation, and violation of their basic human rights (ILO, 2004).

3

Informalization of Labour and Poverty

Poverty has many dimensions of deprivation and denial—social, political, economic, psychological. Therefore, estimates of income and expenditure have limited utility in capturing the depth and range of the deprivation of the impoverished. Where large proportions of the population are subject to high morbidity and mortality, poor access to even minimal healthcare, lack of clean water and sanitation, inadequate housing, lack of education, social exclusion, etc, along with hunger and malnutrition, tend to underestimate the degree of poverty.

The National Commission for Enterprises in the Unorganized Sector, after examining the nature and extent of poverty, concluded (Sengupta, 2008):

> an overwhelming majority of the Indian population, around three-quarters, is poor and vulnerable and it is a staggering 836 million as of 2004–05. This includes 70 million or 6.4 per cent who may be characterised as extremely poor with a per capita consumption of less than or three-quarters of the official poverty line. To this should be added 167 million of those who are poor with consumption not more than that fixed as the official poverty line. If this is relaxed to include those with a per capita consumption of up to 25 per cent above the poverty line, called marginally poor here, then we find another 207 million. These three groups account for 444 million or 40.8 per cent of the population. To this we add those with a per capita

> consumption between 1.25 and two times the poverty line as vulnerable and this group of poor and vulnerable comes to 836 million of Indians or well over 75 per cent of the population. The next major finding is the close association between poverty and vulnerability with one's social identity. The two social groups who are at the bottom by this classification are the SCs/STs, who constitute the bottom layer, and the Muslims, who are in the next layer. This does not mean that the other groups are far better off. The next group is the OBCs, but better than the two bottom layers. Even for those who do not belong to any of these groups, the incidence is 55 per cent. The obverse of this is equally important. It says that in all communities there is a class of better-off, called the middle and high income group, which varies with social identity. Therefore, economic differentiation across social groups is a fact of life in contemporary India, albeit in varying degrees.

In the context of dispossession from lands and natural resources-based livelihoods, an increasing proportion of rural families depend mostly on wage labour for income and survival. Structural maintainers of chronic poverty, especially unequal distribution of land and social hierarchies, remain powerful Chronic Poverty Research Centre, 2007 (Sengupta, 2007). And displacement from employment in the formal sector to unprotected and low wage-paying informal sector meant that a larger proportion of families in urban areas have also been left vulnerable to poverty and deprivation. Most of the families in rural and urban areas also have lack of access to affordable health care. The State's retreat from the health sector and the increasing cost of medical treatment can aggravate vulnerability to acute poverty and deprivation.

Across the country, about 130 million women and men, boys and girls, sleep hungry (Mehta and Shepherd, 2006). The experience of chronic hunger in distant villages as well as on city streets is one of intense avoidable suffering: of self-denial, of learning to live with far less than the body needs; of minds and bodies stymied in their growth; of the agony of helplessly watching one's loved one's—most heartbreakingly children—in hopeless torment; of unpaid, arduous devalued work; of shame, humiliation and bondage; and of the defeat and the triumph of the human spirit.

Such high levels of hunger and malnutrition are a paradox, because they stubbornly survive surging economic growth and agricultural production which outpaces the growth of population (although it has worryingly stagnated in recent years). It is to be stressed here that India has some of the largest and most ambitious food schemes in the world. The persistence of widespread hunger is the cumulative outcome of public policies that produce and reproduce impoverishment; of failures to invest in agriculture, especially in Central and Eastern India (Tata Institute of Social Sciences, 2005); for the rain-fed and small farmers of unacknowledged and unaddressed destitution; and of embedded gender, caste, tribe, disability and stigma, which construct tall social barriers to accessing food. In the last analysis it is the result of a profound collapse of governance.

4

Social Protection in the Context of Acute Distress

Social protection has a crucial role to play in reducing poverty. It tackles the insecurity trap by protecting poor people from shocks and reducing their extreme vulnerability; it helps them conserve and accumulate assets so they can improve their livelihoods and productivity; and it contributes to transforming economic and social relations in ways that strengthen the longer term livelihood prospects of the poor and the chronically poor. While the private, informal and public sectors all have roles to play in providing social protection, the public provision of social protection needs to be prioritized.

India implements massive food, livelihood and social security programmes—some of the largest in the world—which theoretically support vulnerable people from even before their birth to their survivors after death. Expectant mothers are fed in ICDS centres, along with infants, children up to the age of six, and adolescent girls. The child in school gets school meals. As adults, women receive maternity support, bread earners are guaranteed 100 days of wage employment in public works; and if identified to be poor, they can buy subsidized cereals from a massive network of half a million ration shops. The aged—and in many states widows and disabled people as well—are given pensions. And if an earning adult dies prematurely, the survivor is entitled to insurance. India has programmes for all these groups. However, the challenge is to make these programmes work for the poor.

We review two key social protection measures—the National Rural Employment Guarantee Act (NREGA); and the Right to Food program. The renewed pressure to evolve social protection measures to address the threat of chronic malnutrition started in 2001 with the Supreme Court of India (SCI) directing the Government of India (GoI) as part of Citizens Groups petitioning the SCI on this issue. The SCI directed State Governments to bring together a range of subsidized food and supplementary nutrition schemes and programs[1] and placed mechanisms to monitor its implementation. The NREGA of 2005 provides a universal and enforceable legal right to a basic form of employment (in manual labour) at statutory wages and places a judicially enforceable obligation on the State, and gives bargaining power to the workers. The Right to Information Act 2005 provided an instrument to see how government programs are implemented. Currently, the Government is working on a bill to make Right to Food an Act.

NOTES

1. Schemes to ensure food security: The central food schemes and other assistance programmes for the poor in India are: targeted public distribution system; *Antyodaya Anna Yojana*; mid day meal scheme; *Annapoorna Yojana*; integrated child development services; national family benefit scheme; national maternity benefit scheme; and national old age pension scheme.

5

Contextualizing Employment Guarantee

Six decades after Independence, poverty and unemployment in the rural sector remain daunting challenges for India. Emerging problems, in particular agricultural crisis, may potentially thwart sustainability of the economy and society. Although there is a rich history of diverse development interventions by the State and civil society, these initiatives often met with limited success, as it did not translate into a critical mass that would have ameliorated the intimidating impasse couched in entrenched inequalities. It is important to note that these perennial challenges were favorite policy variables under different five-year plans since 1950, while emerging challenges—especially sustainability-related issues—are gaining the attention of the State and civil society. However, it is doubtful if development planning could make strategies which provide solutions by integrating perennial problems and emerging challenges. For instance, barring a few notable exceptions, most of country-wide initiatives have often failed to integrate important variables such as availability of work, public provisioning of food, and protection of natural resources from selfish interests. Moreover, these gaps may evolve to a force that compounds asymmetries such as persistent inequalities, entailing non-tractable complexities in a democratic system.

Given this lineage of development planning, interventions and strategies, the NREGA—seemingly a significant mutation toward an integrated rural development strategy—was initiated by GoI in 2005. This Act guarantees 100 days of employment in a financial year to adult members of any rural household. Initially, this Act covered 200 districts and will be extended to the whole country by 2010. Perhaps, the NREGA can be a structural break in the development trajectory of India, bringing constructive changes. This Act can bring about close to full employment in the rural sector by creating productive assets so as to increase agricultural productivity in a sustainable way, and usher in food security in the country.

Quite importantly, resource allocation for the NREGA can be quite effective if it generates a non-inflationary multiplier process, resulting in an inclusive growth (Shah, 2007). Interestingly, the NREGA has a scholarly genesis—evolving from a model to the stage of policy making. In fact, those who provide a rationale for the NREGA, varying in scope and ideological base, concur that market has no built in capacity to solve unemployment and the resultant asymmetries. One prominent view, propounded by John Maynard Keynes posits that a seemingly stable economy, characterized by equality of aggregate demand and aggregate supply may co-exist with unemployment. Further, such a scenario may trigger off a chain of uncertainties impacting the economy and society. Taking cues from business cycles in the late 1920s, which pervade through industrialized countries, Keynes showed—using the metaphor aggregate or macro economy—that State can be an effective catalyst to attain full employment by injecting investment, which is autonomous of return, to society. As articulated by Keynes, such autonomous investments, through a geometric progression process and known as multiplier, generates a sequence of employment, income and consumption. As assumed by Keynes, these sequences are spontaneous, not subject to any leakages emanating from sources such as corruption. In fact, this logic became an active theme for empirical research, sharply divided about the model's congruence with reality. While lineages defending the Keynesian view promulgate fiscal intervention as a panacea for unemployment, critics—affirming markets' capability to self cure—have been exposing the inefficacy of fiscal strategies to provide sustaining stability.

Interestingly, followed by the early popularity of Keynesian views among industrialized countries, new republics such as India found that this logic would be appropriate to social preferences. Until India transited to an economy which is more open to exogenous variables such as foreign trade and choosing a deregulated market for many goods, services and assets since the 1990s, the Keynesian model greatly impacted its macroeconomic policies, reflected in an expanding public sector, plethora of social sector programmes, subsidy to agriculture, etc. However, with the unleashing of reforms (covering industry, trade and asset markets) in the 1990s, the State's withdrawal from providing support to agriculture and the social sector became quite pronounced. These tendencies to withdraw from welfare orientation and treading through the spontaneity of deregulated markets were fervently pursued by governments since 1990, often aggregated as neo-liberalism. It is important to note that aggregates, which represent macroeconomic sustainability (presumably due to the strategic drift towards neo-liberalism), continue to remain healthy, surviving major external shocks and recessionary forces. For instance, this trend is quite visible in summary measures of balance of payment. Moreover, this trend co-moved with stupendous growth in Gross Domestic Product (GDP) and other macro aggregates.

On the other hand, throughout this period, agricultural productivity, profitability and employment generation steadily decelerated. In fact, rural livelihood became a less important theme for macro strategies, which was a clear departure from the pre-1990s. Interestingly, during 1995–2007, increase in the deregulation of markets co-existed with fractured electoral mandates, leading to a coalitional democracy formed by national and local parties. Quite evidently, during this period, a number of regions became power hubs, in contrast to previous model of high centrality around the Capital City. Perhaps, this dynamics exerted tremendous force to make local problems—in particular agricultural crisis, poverty and unemployment—as the principal determinants of electoral victory. It seems economic buoyancy, once portrayed as the driver of governance, became less important than newly identified determinant of electoral success[1-2] that is, pervading problem such as agricultural crisis, unemployment, poverty, lack of educational attainment, etc.

NREGA: Entitlements and Processes

On assessing the NREGA guidelines given by the GoI, we can classify the entitlements into three: (a) guaranteed employment, (b) entitlement of minimum wage as fixed by the state government, and (c) unemployment benefit. In translating these entitlements into well being, individuals, processes and organizations—including law, government, local government, and grassroot-level organization, play significant roles.

Guaranteed Employment: The NREGA provides an entitlement of 100 days of guaranteed employment in a financial year, targeting households located in an area notified by the GoI. This entitlement is available to more than one adult member of a household,[3] working jointly or at different times. A seeker for this entitlement has to be a local, who resides within the Gram Panchayat (GP). The definition 'local' covers both persons with the domicile status and migrants. It is quite likely an applicant will engage in manual work. It is expected that the Act will cover the whole country by 2010. While this Act's prime focus is on livelihood generation in rural areas, it serves the complementary objective of generating productive assets, protecting the environment, empowering rural women, reducing rural–urban migration and fostering social equity.[4]

Wages: According to the Act, persons who work under the scheme are entitled to minimum wages determined by the state government for agricultural labourers, following the Minimum Wages Act, 1948. Further, complying with the Equal Remuneration Act, 1976, both men and women receive the same wages. The NREGA recommends that wage is to be paid on a weekly basis. Whether these wages are paid the by GP or paid through banks or the local post office, information related to wage is available to the public. If there is a delay in wage payment, workers are entitled to compensation as per the provisions of the Payment of Wages Act, 1936, which shall be borne by the State Government. The NREGA gives the option of social security to persons. If an individual is willing, the State Government may merge the pay with social security arrangements, earmarking a portion of wage to schemes such as health insurance, accident insurance, survivor benefits, maternity benefits, and other social security arrangements.

Unemployment Allowance: If an applicant under the NREGA does not get work within 15 days from the day of application, he/she is entitled to unemployment allowance, to be paid by the State Government. It is important to note that conversion of these entitlements into desired objectives—like the well being of a person—depends, to a greater extent, on the efficacy of processes which enable the functioning of the NREGA. Interestingly, these processes are structured in a spectrum of governance, envisaging tiers of government such as village level, block level, district level, state level and central level. While implementation happens at grassroot units like the village, coordination happens at the block or district level. Moreover, planning and monitoring happens at all levels. Coming to the individual level, the process begins when an individual registers with the GP by providing the required information. After the GP verifies the information, the individual gets a job card, which is valid for five years. If the applicant does not receive a job card, he/she may register grievances about non-issuance of a job card to the program officer. Once an individual gets a job card, the next step is to apply for work. Finally, work is allotted to the applicant.

As given in the NREGA operational guidelines, the scope of work covers works such as:

- water conservation and water harvesting;
- drought proofing, including afforestation and tree plantation;
- irrigation canals, including micro and minor irrigation works;
- provision of irrigation facility to land owned by households belonging to the Scheduled Caste/ Scheduled Tribe, or to land of the beneficiaries of land reforms, or to land of the beneficiaries under the Indira Awas Yojana;
- renovation of traditional water bodies, including de-silting of tanks;
- land development, flood-control and protection works, including drainage in waterlogged areas; and
- rural connectivity to provide all-weather access.

Clearly, these works aim to generate productive assets in rural areas, which may rejuvenate the rural economy[5].

NREGA: Current Scene

Although a balanced assessment of the NREGA's ability to attain desired objectives needs a longer time horizon, policy commentators, academic scholars and other observers, have been sharing their views on its likely direction. While some views position the NREGA as an inevitable choice for India, contrary to this view, some commentators observe the NREGA as a fiscal profligacy[6]. However, giving an assessment of the first two years (Table 1), Drèze and Christian (2009) feel that processes of the NREGA are yet to attain desirable level of responsiveness, particularly in sharing data about its progress.

Commenting on the less satisfactory state of the art database, Drèze and Christian (2009) observe:

Table 1: NREGA Fact Sheet

	"Phase I" Districts Only (2006-07)	*"Phase I" Districts Only (2007-08)*	*Phase I + Phase II Districts*
Number of Districts under NREGA	200	200	330
Person-days of employment generated			
Total (crore)	90	108	144
Per household	17	20	16
Per job card	24	25	22
Per household employed in NREGA	43	48	42
Share of marginalized groups in NREGA employment (per cent)			
Women	40	44	42
Scheduled Tribe (ST)	36	33	29
Scheduled Caste (SC)	26	27	27
Expenditure on NREGA			
Total Expenditure (Rs. Crore)	8813	12057	15857
Average Expenditure per district (Rs. Crore)	44	60	48
Average expenditure per person-day	98	111	110
Average wage cost per-person day	65	75	75
Share of wages in Total Expenditure (%)	66	67	68

Source: Drèze and Christian (2009)

"the accuracy of the official figures is an open question, which calls for urgent scrutiny. In any case, independent large-scale surveys of the NREGA (analogous to, say, the National Family Health Survey) would be very useful.... It is worth noting that there are crucial gaps in the present "Monitoring and Information System" (MIS). This is one reason why long delays in wage payments persist in many States, causing immense hardship to NREGA workers and even inducing some of them to "quit". These and other gaping holes in the statistical system need urgent attention if the NREGA is to achieve its ambitious transparency norms."

Ambasta et al. (2008) identified five major shortcomings of the implementation of the NREGA: (i) lack of professionals, (ii) delay in administration, (iii) under-staffing, (iv) inappropriate schedule of rates, and (v) mockery of social audit. Quite visibly, these shortcomings can snowball to compounding of transaction costs, which may thwart the sustainability of NREGA.[7]

NOTES

1. Chandrasekhar and Ghosh (2004) affirming the role of employment in electoral results: "There is no doubt that employment generation has emerged as not only the most important socio-economic issue in the country today, but also the most pressing political concern. The mandate of the recent elections is clear on this: the people of the country have decisively rejected policies that have implied reduced employment opportunities and reduced access to, and quality of, public goods and services."
2. Analysis (Rudra, 2002) shows that there are political factors (such as strong labor power and democracy) that can positively affect welfare spending in this era of globalization. Welfare-state retrenchment is a consequence of the failure of politics to intervene in the economy. Minimizing the trade-off between thriving capitalism and social welfare in developing economies can be accomplished through greater political and institutional development. Labor's political influence ultimately depends on workers' ability to organize and the capacity to affect electoral outcomes. Thus, an important challenge facing LDCs today is to reconcile international competitiveness with a democratic environment that allows autonomous labor market institutions to flourish.
3. As given by Ministry of Rural Development (2005), 'household' means a nuclear family comprising mother, father, and their

children, and may include any person wholly or substantially dependent on the head of the family. Household will also mean a single-member family.'

4. Ministry of Rural Development (2005) states that "the basic objective of the Act is to enhance livelihood security in rural areas by providing at least 100 days of guaranteed wage employment in a financial year to every household whose adult members volunteer to do unskilled manual work. This work guarantee can also serve other objectives: generating productive assets, protecting the environment, empowering rural women, reducing rural–urban migration and fostering social equity, among others".
5. Ghosh (2004) expresses optimism: "Such a scheme—which would dramatically improve the material condition of the rural poor while at the same time increasing capital formation and productivity in rural India—is clearly in the best interests of the country as a whole."
6. Drèze (2004) sees the Employment Guarantee Act as an enforceable obligation on the State. However, Acharya (2009) expresses concern that the NREGA can be an irreversible expenditure item, causing fiscal stress to the economy.
7. State and sub-state political economy also often leads to poor performance of rural development schemes, which are notoriously prone to "leakage" into a bureaucrat-contractor-village leader nexus, thereby restricting their potential to boost agricultural growth. However, some progress on these problems can be observed. Electoral competition has driven the government to focus on poverty more recently. And movements at the grassroots, such as the Mazdoor Kisan Shakti Sanghathan (MKSS) in Rajasthan and other "right to information" campaigns, have played a part in extending and deepening democratic politics beyond urban and literate classes. In some areas, they have exposed the corruption and inefficiency of poorly-performing schemes, even to the point of seeing corrupt officials pay back embezzled funds. At the state and national levels, anti-poverty programmes have been subject to redesign and change in recent years. For example, even in Orissa, which remains one of the poorest states in monetary terms, notable improvements in human development indicators such as child malnutrition, infant mortality and

literacy have been achieved. Several schemes have undergone reforms, rationalisation and better targeting with a greater role for local government in implementation and for beneficiary selection and monitoring, a stress on transparency, making information available at the village level, and on social audits. These points to the tremendous positive potential of better central–local cooperation and the mobilisation of poorer people. However, while these reforms are very welcome, there is still a long way to go.

6

Right to Food

The most evolved definition of food security appears in the State of Food Insecurity 2001 (Commissioners of the Supreme Court of India, 2008): "Food security [is] a situation that exists when all people, at all times, have physical, *social* and economic access to sufficient, safe and nutritious food that meets their dietary needs and food preferences for an active and healthy life". The inclusion in the definition of 'social' access is highly significant, because it acknowledges that people may be barred from access to food even if it is locally available and they have the economic means. These social barriers to food security may include gender, caste, race, disability or stigmatised ailments.

In India, food security exists at the macro level in terms of physical access to food. Economic access is far from satisfactory, both at the micro as well as at the macro level. The statement that economic access to food is far from satisfactory is confirmed by the fact that a significant proportion of society lives in poverty and is malnourished. This section of the society is underprivileged and has less voice. The question that arises is: who will ensure food security for the underprivileged? Is it the state, the market or the civil society or a combination of all three? The framework of right to food is one of the basic economic and social rights that are essential to achieve 'economic democracy' without which political democracy is, at best, incomplete (Cheriyan, 2006).

It is interesting to note that four employment generation programs initiated by the GoI have been linked with provisioning of food and nutrition, targeting poor, drought-affected areas, and with objectives such as development of human resources and food security (Table 2). It is important to note that the linkage between food and work is quite a fundamental one. Moreover, the nutritional value of food is a principal factor in this linkage.

Magnifying this linkage, Ray (2006, p. 272) expresses: "Because under nutrition affects the capacity to work, it affects the functioning of labour markets in a central way." As shown by Ray, work capacity tends to have a non-linear relation with nutrition. While work capacity tends to be abysmally low for low nutrition levels, the former increases at an increasing rate for subsequent units of nutrition, until the curve reaches a point of inflexion. Beyond this point, the curve increases at a declining rate until it reaches saturation point. It is important to note that nearly one-fourth of married men and slightly above half of married women, in the age

Table 2: Integrating Food with Employment Programmes

Programme	*Period*	*Objective in relation to food*
Food for Work Programme	1977-1980	Utilize surplus food grain for the development for human resources
National Rural Employment Programme (NREGP)	1980-1989	Raise nutritional standard of the poor.
Food for Work Programme II	2000-2002	Augment food security through wage employment in draught affected rural areas.
Sampoorna Grameen Rozgar Yojana (SGRY)	2001	Food security

Source: Table 2.1, p. 5, Second Administrative Reforms Commission (2006)

group of 15–49 are anemic (Ministry of Health and Family Welfare, 2005–2006), implying lower work capacity for the economically active population in India. Obviously, to a significant extent, the demographic dividend emanating from the economically active population in India greatly depends on this segment's capacity to engage in both economic and non-economic activities. Further, this link is significantly directed by the availability of nutritious food, either free or at affordable prices.

Responding to this scenario, GoI issued the Citizen Charter in November 1997, aiming to make functioning of the Public Distribution System (PDS) more transparent and accountable. This Charter contains information on themes such as entitlement of Below Poverty Line (BPL) families, quality of food grains, and procedure for the issue of ration cards inspection and checking, information regarding fair price shops, right to information, vigilance and public participation. In 2007, the Charter underwent a revision; the revised model citizens' charter replaced the old charter.[1] Interestingly, the revised Charter places significantly great weight on defining the target population and operational aspects, while less emphasis is given on aspects such as distribution of more nutritious food to all segments of population, covering children, ageing population and economically active population. As shown by Virmani and Rajeev (2001), demand for higher quality food has been steadily going up in India, while the PDS still centers around cereals[2]. Further, Hanumantha Rao (cited by Virmani and Rajeev), attributes the change in preference to factors such as spread of the road network to rural areas and the increased availability of manufactured goods in rural areas.[3] The excess supply of cereals, contrary to preference for better quality food, often results in excess stocks in the PDS. It is doubtful if there have been constructive attempts to devise a right to quality food, which can raise the capacity to sustain and work.

This scenario is echoed by India Vision 2020, released in 2002 (Planning Commission, 2002), which says that India is going to have the capacity to produce more than sufficient quantities of food to provide a healthy diet to its entire population and become a major food exporter well before 2020. However, the Report is doubtful if this is enough for eradicating under-nutrition. "In spite of enormous progress in the food production, nearly half the country's population still suffers from chronic under-nutrition and malnutrition. The most vulnerable are children, women and the elderly among the lower income groups".

The Report states that it is important to increase the purchasing power of people by generating livelihoods, which would enable people to consume nutritious food. While enumerating this link, the Report notes that

> "Employment or livelihood security is an essential and inseparable element of a comprehensive strategy for national food security. Conversely, food security is an essential requirement for raising the productivity of India's workforce to international levels... The problem of chronic macro and micro nutrient under-nutrition cannot be addressed simply by increases in food production or the accumulation of larger food buffer stocks. Nor has the public distribution system been able to effectively target the neediest in an effective manner. Targeted food for work programmes and targeted nutrition programmes can alleviate the problem temporarily. But in the long run, the solution is to ensure employment opportunities for all citizens so that they acquire the purchasing power to meet their nutritional requirements. Thus, employment or livelihood security becomes an essential and inseparable component of a comprehensive strategy for national food security and must be considered as one of the nation's highest priorities."

NOTES

1. See http://fcamin.nic.in/dfpd_html/index.asp
2. Citing them, "Between 1972/73 and 1993/94 the food basket has become much more diversified. In particular, cereal shares have seen a dramatic decline of ten percentage points in most

of regions—in both rural and urban India. Similarly, the share of meat and milk products, and vegetables and fruits has increased over time." (p. 2)

3. Reflecting on this change, Virmani and Rajeev note (p. 3), "People today prefer to consume more of non-cereals and among cereals the preference is for rice and wheat as against coarse cereals. There is a shift in the consumption pattern of the population in favour of superior food items like milk, vegetables, fruits, and animal foods. Thus the growth of aggregate demand for cereals in the country is slowing down because of deceleration in the pace of population growth and a shift in consumer preference towards non-cereals. This is one of the factors that have contributed to accumulation of excessive food stocks in FCI godowns."

7

Conclusion: Making Social Protection Measures Work for the Poor

These programs are plagued by corruption, leakages, errors in selection, delays, poor allocations and little accountability. They also tend to discriminate against and exclude those who need them the most—by social barriers of gender, age, caste, ethnicity, faith and disability; and State hostility to urban poor migrants, street and slum residents, and unorganised workers. Political support and long-term commitment are key to making them work. Often the demand for work and food remain poorly articulated when faced with political and administrative indifferences (Chronic Poverty Research Centre, 2007). In democratic politics, political officials have incentives to incorporate voters' preferences into welfare policies to reduce the risk of electoral loss (for themselves or for members of their party), and also the risk of public reprisal in the form of civil disobedience or protests.

Cues from observations such as the above, clearly hint that right to food is not just a transient food security[1] built around building excess supply of cereals, but is more a dynamic one, which absorbs the population's demand for a food basket, having a direct linkage with health, capacity to work and sustenance. Undoubtedly, a dynamic approach to rights would entail bundling of right to education, right to work, right to health and right to food, and strengthening of

Right to Information, the principle accountability enhancing mechanism.

NOTES

1. See Radhakrishna and Venkata Reddy (2002)

References

Acharya, S. (2009): "Fiscal stimulus or fiscal ruin", *Business Standard*, 9 July.

Ambasta, P., Vijay Shankar, P.S. and Shah, M. (2008): "Two years of NREGA: the road ahead", *Economic and Political Weekly*, 23 February, pp. 41–50.

Chandrasekhar, C.P. and Ghosh, J. (2004): "How feasible is a rural employment guarantee", *Business Line*, Tuesday, 22 June.

Chronic Poverty Research Centre (2007): "Chronic Poverty in India: Policy Responses", Policy Brief No. 4, March.

Cheriyan, G. (2006): Enforcing the Right to Food in India: Bottlenecks in Delivering the Expected Outcome, Research Paper No. 2006/132, November, UNU, WIDER.

Commissioners of the Supreme Court (2008). Eighth Report of the Commissioners of the Supreme Court. "A Special Report on Most Vulnerable Social Groups and Their Access to Food" In the case: PUCL v. UOI & Ors. Writ Petition (Civil) No. 196 of 2001, August 2008.

Drèze, J. (2004): "Employment as a social responsibility", *The Hindu*, 22 November.

Drèze, J. and Oldiges, C. (2009): "Work in Progress", *Frontline*, Vol. 26, No. 04, February, pp. 14–27.

Ghosh, J. (2004): "Rural employment as policy priority", *Frontline*, Vol. 21, No.14, July, pp. 03–16.

International Labour Organization (2004): "A Fair Globalization: Creating Opportunities For All". The World Commission on the Social Dimension of Globalization.

Mausam (2008): "The climate crisis and people's struggles", Vol. 1, No.1, July–September.

Mehta, A. and Shepherd, A. (eds.) (2006): "*Chronic Poverty and Development Policy in India*", New Delhi: Sage Publications.

Ministry of Rural Development (2005), National Rural Employment Guarantee Act 2005, Operational Guidelines, New Delhi: Government of India.

Ministry of Health and Family Welfare (2005–2006): National Family Health Survey (NFHS-3), New Delhi: Government of India

Planning Commission (2002): "India Vision 2020", New Delhi: Government of India.

Radhakrishna and Venkata Reddy (2002): "Food Security and Nutrition: Vision 2020", New Delhi: Planning Commission, Government of India.

Ray, D. (2006): "*Development Economics*", Delhi: Oxford University Press.

Rudra, N. (2002): "Globalization and the Decline of the Welfare State in Less-Developed Countries", *International Organization*, Vol. 56, No. 2 (Spring), pp. 411–445.

Sanyal, K. and Bhattacharya, R. (2009): "Beyond the Factory: Globalisation, Informalisation of Production and the New Locations of Labour", *Economic & Political Weekly*. Vol. 46, No. 22.

Second Administrative Reforms Commission (2006): "Unlocking human capital: entitlements and governances: A case study", New Delhi: Government of India.

Sengupta, Arjun, Kannan, K.P. and Raveendran, G. (2008): India's Common People: Who Are They, How Many Are They and How Do They Live?, *Economic & Political Weekly*, March 15, 2008.

Shah, M. (2007): "Employment Guarantee, civil society and Indian democracy", *Economic and Political Weekly*, November 17, pp. 43–51.

Tata Institute of Social Sciences, (2005): "Causes of Suicide among the Farmers in Maharashtra", Report to the Bombay High Court, Mumbai.

Virmani, A. and Rajeev, P. (2001): "Excess food stocks, PDS and procurement policy", Working Paper No 5/2002, New Delhi: Planning Commission, Government of India.